FRIENDS FROM THE FOREST

JOY ADAMSON

FRIENDS from the FOREST

With a Foreword by
JULIETTE HUXLEY

A Helen and Kurt Wolff Book
Harcourt Brace Jovanovich, Publishers
New York and London

Library of Congress Cataloging in Publication Data

Adamson, Joy.
Friends from the forest.

"A Helen and Kurt Wolff book."
Contents: Colobus monkeys—Verreaux's eagle owls.
1. Colobus.   2. Verreaux's eagle owl.   I. Title.
QL737.P93A3   1981   599.8'2   81-47295
ISBN 0-15-133645-8   AACR2

Printed in the United States of America

B C D E

CONTENTS

Foreword *by Juliette Huxley*   xi

PART I   Colobus Monkeys   3

PART II   Verreaux's Eagle Owls   39

Postscript   75

ILLUSTRATIONS

Colobus monkeys between pages   12 and 13
Verreaux's eagle owls between pages   44 and 45

Since Joy Adamson could no longer provide
captions for the photographs, these have been
captioned only where indications in the text
allowed at least tentative identification.

FOREWORD

Julian and I first met the Adamsons in 1960, on our long voyage from Cape Town to Uganda. Quoting from my book *Wild Lives of Africa* revives the memories of those days:

> In the bungalow on the other side of Isiolo we met Joy Adamson. She is Austrian by birth, has a small round face, brown as a berry, a tiny nose, fair hair in curls round her head, and wears her neat figure well. Having admired her book *Born Free*, I knew she must be a person of character and firmness. She certainly was—promptly took charge of our needs and supplied us with everything, including lunch.
>
> Words came tumbling out, enthusiastic, irrepressible.
>
> George Adamson looks just like his

photographs, with a short pointed beard and bright blue eyes with the piercing vision of hunters and sailors.

We read the story of Elsa, as almost everyone did at that time, and were naturally anxious to see her. But there was a snag. A distinguished visitor, recently camping out with the Adamsons in order to make the acquaintance of Elsa, had on two successive nights been strangely visited by her, in spite of the lioness-proof boma built around his tent. But Elsa was not an ordinary lioness, and George had to break in, with his gun, to shoo her off.

Understandably, Joy was much disturbed. Our request was met with a firm refusal. A lot of persuasion was needed to bend her will, and when at last she consented, it was with the proviso that we would not get out of the Land Rover, nor make our presence in any way felt as an intrusion by Elsa.

Two Land Rovers took us to the rendezvous where Elsa could be tempted to come with her cubs, a goat being provided to show our good intentions. George shot in the air, and after a short while Elsa came bounding out of the bush, nearly knocking Joy down in the exuberance of her affectionate greeting. We felt very frustrated locked up in the cab, but we had promised.

I was lucky to be sitting next to Joy on our journeys there and back, and became almost more interested in her than in Elsa. She relaxed in the most friendly manner and, discussing Elsa, revealed much of herself. She had adopted the baby lioness with great patience and sustained attention—feeding her always from her hands—for animals, unlike human beings, seldom bite the hand that feeds them. Elsa became the child she had never had—three miscarriages having ended all hopes of true maternity for her—and she spent on the little creature all the maternal love she had. George encouraged and guided her all through, for what was an instinctive approach in Joy was factual knowledge in him.

We had been deeply impressed by the whole experience—not only of seeing with our own eyes the trustful bond which bound together a wild animal and two dedicated human beings, but by the Adamsons themselves.

Throughout the years we kept up with each other—Julian wrote the preface to Joy's second book, *Living Free*—and we followed their adventures with great interest. In November 1976, having attended the UNESCO Celebrations in Nairobi, I got in touch with Joy and she invited me to Naivasha.

Elsamere is a modest bungalow within large and lovely grounds planted with many roses and exotics, facing the blue waters of Lake Naivasha through a screen of fever trees. Joy had furnished it with the minimum—her bedroom had a bed in one corner, a wide empty space, and a wall of built-in closets to house her clothes and various possessions. A glassed-in veranda opened through her windows; her table stood there with its typewriter and working materials; and she spent much time writing and watching the outside world from this peaceful place. There was a library with armchairs and bookshelves, a dining room, two more bedrooms—also sparsely furnished—and two bathrooms. The kitchen was very plain and sober, inhabited by a surly African who was the only attendant indoors.

The wild forest—a small remnant of the original fringes of that enchanting lake—surrounded the estate and was full of friendly animals who visited Joy, enjoying the fruit and vegetables always available and showing no fear or suspicion of her, though still ready to fly off at the sight of unusual visitors. Just in front of the veranda was a large enclosure where animals, occasionally brought to recover from troubles, were devotedly nursed by Joy. This enclosure was later used to keep Penny, the baby leopard.

Yet, for all its peace and its idyllic situation, a sense of loneliness brooded over Elsamere. Joy had by then suffered many accidents, her right hand was so damaged that she could no longer use it for painting, though she trained her left sufficiently well to paint a fine portrait of the Verreaux's eagle owl she writes about in this book. Her hip was broken—then her right elbow, then her leg and right knee—and finally her right arm was in trouble.

She had great physical courage, and endured these grave handicaps with an angry disregard for the need of crutches and plaster casts, hobbling

around the trees where the Colobus monkeys met her, descending to her call—or the Verreaux's eagle owl waited for her coming with the chicken heads she fed it. All her books, the papers she wrote recently on these fascinating creatures, reflect her infinite patience and absorption in whatever observation she had undertaken, and the deep joy these contacts with wild animals gave her. As I watched her at Elsamere, feeding the Colobus with gentle care, I realized how she herself was nourished by their trust in her.

Such a trust can only be given by the persistent denial of the human self to the alert suspicious awareness of the animal: it could be a long and slow vigil until the instinctive fear is subdued and the animal takes the initial step nearer, and another, and finally allows human contact.

Joy had learned to persevere infinitely in these long hours of preparation, leading eventually to bonds of acceptance. She was, perhaps, more delicately aware of the need of such patience to communicate with wild animals than in her relations with human beings. She could be quick tempered, expecting more understanding than she was prepared to give.

In spite of the remarkable success she achieved her wild flower paintings, her portraits of tribal notables and documentation of their regalia, her immense contribution to the conservation of wild life all over the world—donating the fortune she made

from books, films, and lectures—Joy was a child. And a child she remained all her life, a willful, unreasonable child.

During my stay with her, Joy arranged fascinating trips to the Aberdares and specially to Nakuru, the flamingo lake. It was while we were stuck in the rich smelly guano, her large car axle-deep in the ooze, watching a superb sunset streaked with the bright pink and black of flamingos flying home, and waiting for the help searched for by the two friends who had accompanied us, that we talked of many things, our problems past, present, and future.

Her loneliness was deeply disturbing—the last years of her life shadowed by disappointments and loss of friends. Her firm chin denoted the animating willpower, a willpower sometimes excessive to circumstances not amenable to its demands. In her deep love and concern for nature she was intensely ambitious and resented obstacles in her way. If she made enemies in her attempts to pursue some carefully planned study, she did so with a conviction that her way was the only proper way, and should win assent and support from all concerned. She could not accept resistance; it only aroused her fighting spirit and determination.

By now, the sun had set on Lake Nakuru, and a soft darkness enveloped all. Birds folded their wings, ceasing their chattering—and Joy and I fell silent in the magic of the moment. It was then we became aware of a strange phenomenon: from the

soft crust of the guano beneath our sunken wheels clouds of small black flies flew up, in millions, penetrating the car, clinging to hair and faces, and emanating a strong, persistent scent of incense, a scent which dominated and extinguished the guano stink.

It was the mating season of the insects—three nights a year, when they rise out of their long incubation to seek their mates, signaling their presence and their urgency with what is called pheromones. To me, it was a good omen, a promise of better things to come for Joy, now in the distress of frustration as well as in the persistent battering of her bones, the failing of her hitherto indestructible health.

And indeed it was that very day, at Lake Nakuru, almost by chance but how providentially, that she heard for the first time of the orphan female leopard cub for which she had been waiting. She had the highest hopes of taming and studying this most difficult of wild creatures, and possibly repeating the moving story of Elsa. One felt that this ambitious venture, at this moment of her extraordinary life, and need, was immensely important, a veritable lifeline. And when later I heard that she had secured the baby leopard, and taken her to the bush to begin her training and observation, I rejoiced that her chance had come at last.

Her loving study of Penny was finished. She had handed in the manuscript just before Christmas; like all her books, a great achievement of patient observation, and a triumph of creating a bond of understanding and trust between a dangerous, rarely tamed creature and a human being. It was Joy's most difficult and unpredictable experience, and her real success must have given her a deep sense of achievement.

Her strange death by murder was a grievous shock. But can we know if, in her unhappy and troubled heart, physically exhausted and worried by her brittle bones, she did not apprehend her precarious future and dream of death as a refuge?

And it happened in the peaceful hour of her evening walk, enjoying a communion with nature, which was her way of knowing God. As she wrote in her autobiography:

> I had traveled across Africa, the U.S.A., Canada, Europe, Asia, Australia, New Zealand, and Japan, speaking to people on behalf of endangered wildlife. I had received many high awards. Now I wondered how all this could have happened, for I felt I had changed very little since the summer days at Seifenmühle when we children played at lion hunts. My ideas are the same as they have always been. For instance: I believe today as I did then that God is in every ray of sunshine, in the song of every bird, in the rustle of the wind and the flicker of the setting sun turning the country into gold. All this means more to me than any candle in a cathedral, and I still have no need to dress

up to meet God on Sunday in a church, for I can talk to him at any moment, as to my closest friend.

Would she have called her end a blessing, a strangely fitting end for her *Searching Spirit*?

JULIETTE HUXLEY

FRIENDS FROM THE FOREST

PART ONE

Colobus Monkeys

I HAD ALWAYS BEEN FASCINATED BY BLACK-AND-white Colobus monkeys, which, in my opinion, are the most handsome of all monkeys. Indeed, when they are leaping through the trees with outstretched arms, their long white and black hair trailing like a veil behind them, they look more like fairy creatures than monkeys.

Zoologically they belong to one of the ten subspecies of *Colobus guereza*, which together with the twelve subspecies of *Colobus polykomos* are the two main species of the black-and-white Colobus. All are arboreal and occur only in Africa. In spite of their striking appearance, comparatively little is known about their habits because they are extremely difficult to observe amid the dense foliage of the forests and they are masters of the art of concealment. Nothing is known about the gestation, the sexual behavior, or the lifespan of *Colobus guereza kikuyuensis* living wild; the only record we have is from the San Diego Zoo, where one lived for twenty-four years.

Colobus (*Kolobos*, in Greek) means "mutilated" and refers to the thumb—it is virtually absent, being represented by a small bump or tubercle.

These gregarious, arboreal primates live in groups in territories averaging 0.037 square miles, which is small compared to those of terrestrial monkeys.

Each group is dominated by a male who spends most of the day on the lookout and utters a deep, sonorous roar when out of sight of the rest of the group. Peter Marler suggests that "its primary function is to maintain territorial spacing of groups, but not the actual territorial defence. Troops of mixed sexes have well-defined territories which coincide roughly with the home range (the home range is the area in which the troops move during the year; the territory is that part of the home range which is actively defended through repulsion of intruding troops by vocalisation, display, or combat)."

R. Schenkel stresses the importance of the roar in group cohesion, "showing who is boss" and maintaining the hierarchy. The roar can be heard for over a mile and may last up to twenty minutes; it is broken into sequences lasting five to fifteen seconds. The roar is unique among those of primates, except for that of the Howler monkey *Alouatta villosa* in Central America, which also has, according to Schenkel, "striking social and ecological similarities with *Colobus guereza*. Both species inhabit a canopy of primary forest and are mainly leaf-eaters; both live in stable exclusive groups with marked internal intimacy, and show group territoriality and a special far-reaching choric display. There are, however, important differences in these respective displays. Whereas in the Howler, the whole group takes part in the chorus, in Colobus, the dominant male represents his group and has, in this respect, a unique and prominent position within the group."

Marler informs us, "The sexes can be identified by the white patch below the tail which is a complete ring in males and a broken ring in females."

Colobus kikuyuensis normally live in the forests at altitudes of between 7,000 and 9,000 feet; so I was surprised and thrilled when I found a pair at Elsamere, our new home on Lake Naivasha, which is at an altitude of 6,200 feet. They probably came from the nearby hills in some dry season, to take advantage of the luscious lakeside vegetation; then perhaps they were stranded at Elsamere when the neighboring forest was cut down. However, they seem to have adapted well to the climate and vegetation. They feed on the juicy leaves of a senecio climber, the leaves of the acacia, and those of an imported pepper tree; other favorites are leaves from the undergrowth. Usually the monkeys keep strictly to the security of the high trees where they are safe from leopards and other tree-climbing predators.

While we were watching our pair feed high up in a tree, the branch on which one was sitting broke

7

and the monkey landed with a thud on the ground. Luckily it fell onto the lawn between two rocks. Though it had fallen about 100 feet, it jumped up immediately, ran up the tree, and then disappeared with its mate. Next day I saw both of them again, and, as far as I could judge, they behaved normally. After this they departed for sixteen days, and I could not trace them. I feared that the one who had fallen might have been injured or even have died. I was therefore relieved when I discovered the pair deep in the forest. One of the hands of the female seemed to be purple, and she sat hunched up and immobile. Then when I looked at her through my field glasses I discovered that her "injured hand" was the face of a baby.

Later I saw a pure-white tail about five inches long, dangling from beneath the mother's arm. She clutched the infant close to her body with one arm while handling herself along the trunk with the other until she reached the top of the tree. The father followed her and remained within a few feet of his family, watching me closely.

It was a happy anticlimax to my anxiety to see the pair not only unharmed, but with a baby that I knew had been born between June 3 and 18, 1970. It was completely white, except for its pale-purple face, and was less than a foot long, with a straight tail of the same length as its body.

The parents, especially the father, were very nervous during the next few days. Whenever he saw me, he sat straight up, ready to protect his family. Sometimes the mother would move up to him, putting her head into his lap while the youngster crawled clumsily over her. When she went, usually into the undergrowth, to feed, she gripped the infant close while the father kept guard high up in the branches and called often to his mate.

After ten days little Coli, as I named the baby, had developed black ears which matched his large black eyes. It was then that for the first time the family, though very apprehensive, risked leaving the forest and going into the trees that faced the house. A week later I saw for the first time Coli moving a few inches away from his mother. She hung on to him until he struggled back and sat on her head. This could not have been comfortable for her; nevertheless, she kept absolutely still until Coli again ventured a foot away to explore a branch of senecio. Then she again grabbed him, jumped onto a thin branch, and swung around a few times until he got a good grip; now Coli clung firmly to her belly.

Assuming that he was born around June 10, he was now about one month old. He had developed a dark patch on his forehead, his tail had grown thick at the end, and his face had turned gray.

Just then I had to leave Elsamere for a month, as I wanted to search in Meru National Park for the cubs of my cheetah, Pippa. On my return I found that Coli's hands and feet had become black, his arms and face were gray, and his forehead was divid-

9

ed from the lower part of his face by a thin white line. The rest of his body was still pure white and his tail had a distinct tassel.

The father seemed extremely nervous and always remained a few yards above his family while Coli and his mother sat for long spells close together, gazing at and caressing each other. Within another two weeks Coli's head had turned black and I saw him eating leaves.

The affection between mother and child seemed to be increasing day by day. Often I saw the mother push leaves into Coli's mouth or lift his legs to groom him; then suddenly she would stop while they hugged each other. The father always sat at a little distance away, keeping a lookout for danger.

The young monkey's coloring changed rapidly; within two months and three weeks his arms, legs, face, and belly had turned gray and his forehead, feet, and hands were black. His head was now the size of an orange. He munched leaves with gusto while still suckling his mother (her teats were one inch long)—at least that was what he seemed to be doing, though he may have been merely getting comfort. Afterward Coli would hop away, jump around, or dangle from twigs before somersaulting at the queerest angles back to his mother. In some invisible way she apparently controlled his exercises, for occasionally she spanked him when, evidently, he had not obeyed her.

Soon the little fellow was black all over, except for the long cape around his back (which was gray), the white mask around his face (which covered his throat up to behind his ears), and his white tail.

The family was now quite used to us and remained placidly in the trees when we were around, but when visitors came it made for the forest. The rains were a new experience for Coli, but he seldom got wet: for most of the time his mother covered him with her arms, spreading her cape protectively around his body. It was interesting to see the way in which the family climbed to the tops of the trees when a storm was heavy. I assumed they did this to avoid falling branches.

They had their favorite trees on which they would feed and rest, or which they would use when crossing their territory. This extended for about one mile within the borders of our property, and sometimes even beyond our forest to my neighbor's trees.

I had always believed that a monkey's ability to jump safely was innate, but now when I watched the parents sitting at a short distance from each other and Coli hopping to and fro between them, I realized that they were gradually widening the distance. Coli often used their shoulders as a jumping board, preferring his mother's—probably because he could slide across her hunched-up back, whereas his father did not hunch so conveniently. This was the first time I noticed the father taking an active part in his son's education.

While these lessons went on the Colobus kept silent. It was in the early morning that the father usually gave voice; he would first make a clicking sound with his tongue and lower his head and body before uttering the deep, sonorous roar characteristic of the Colobus; while doing this he jerked his head repeatedly. The mother roared only on a few occasions, for a shorter time and at a much lower volume than her mate. When the small monkey was in trouble he uttered a squeak, whereupon the parent who was nearest always rushed to his rescue.

I had to go again to Meru National Park. When I came back I saw that Coli's color was just like that of an adult, though his coat was not yet as glossy and it was still rather fluffy. He was then around five and a half months old.

He was by now able to jump quite far from his mother; but when alarmed he instantly rushed to her, and she would clutch him to her belly, carrying him off to release him at a safe distance.

The family was very active in the morning, when they combined playing and feeding. When the sun got warm, around eleven-thirty, they retired to the top of a tree to sleep. About four in the afternoon they resumed feeding; this lasted till dusk. Then they went high up a tree to sleep through the night.

During the daytime Coli was a very busy little monkey. He loved dangling by one arm from a branch, twirling around and around; and he enjoyed swinging to and fro while holding on with both hands, clutching a twig, or hopping up and down on a branch just for the fun of it. His father sometimes

Joy Adamson feeding the orphans

played with him. Occasionally Coli became bold and swung a branch against one of his parents or even pulled at a leaf one of them was eating; for this he was always spanked. Once I even saw him spanking his mother; but then, knowing that he was asking for trouble, he quickly hopped across her head, out of reach of her well-aimed smack.

Although Coli was now pretty well independent of his parents, he was still unable to climb his favorite acacia tree, which had a trunk a foot in diameter; acacias have a very smooth bark, so he could not get a good grip on it and inevitably fell back after gaining a few feet. Finally his mother came to his rescue. Placing herself in a fork two feet above him, she let her tail hang down, and Coli, using it as a rope ladder, heaved himself up to her. If his mother could not help him for lack of a convenient fork, Coli shinned up a thinner neighboring tree, and then he jumped from its top into the tree where his parents were and slid backward down the smooth trunk until he could join them. Twice I watched the male clambering up the tree to meet Coli, who then used his father's shoulders as a springboard to cover a greater distance.

On the whole, the father was far more wary of me than the mother, who had learned to trust me and allowed me to come within ten yards of her to take photographs. I wished that Coli were as cooperative as she, but whenever he saw me focusing the camera on him, he hopped behind a tree, peeped around it to see if I was still there, and kept in hiding until I lost patience; then as soon as I had turned my back he came into view again, posing in the funniest positions.

My next visit to Meru National Park lasted for three weeks. I returned on the evening of August 13 to learn that one of the Colobus parents had been missing for two weeks. Early next morning we all started searching. On the last afternoon we spotted a Colobus high up in a tree, close to the boundary of my forest. He was still, and one arm was hanging down. He was dead. There was no sign of the rest of the family. Two fish eagles sat on a tree close by.

Suddenly we heard two gun shots from the direction of my neighbor's property. Fearing for the lives of the two surviving monkeys, I sent one of my men to investigate. On his return he told me that the owner was away and that the staff had said he had no right to question them as they were only target shooting. One does not practice target shooting with a shotgun; that was how they were armed, so my suspicion that they had killed the Colobus was strengthened. Meanwhile, we tried to get the body down, but we found it impossible to climb the smooth bark of the acacia and had to postpone the gruesome task until the next day.

What had this endearing monkey done to deserve being killed, probably by a poacher hoping to be paid a pittance for the skin or to sell the tail as a fly switch? Colobus are highly protected animals, and, besides, the monkey had been killed on my property, where nobody is allowed to shoot without my permission.

Next morning we took three bamboo poles, each about eight yards long; by tying them together we managed to reach the carcass and eventually succeeded in pushing the body off the tree. After we had recovered it we found an empty cartridge case nearby in the thick undergrowth.

The body was almost mummified, except for the eyes, which looked hauntingly alive. Even in death the father was both beautiful and dignified. His head was bent backward, and one arm clung to a branch. He must have been killed instantly. We carried him to the house, where I examined the body carefully. It was riddled with shotgun pellets. Since I might need evidence for the police and the Game Department, who would investigate the crime, I photographed the victim and cut the tail off before burying the body near the house at the edge of the forest.

Then I went in search of Coli and his mother. I found them on the tree where earlier I had seen the fish eagles. Coli was clinging to his mother.

I called the local police and the Game Department in Nairobi. Their searches revealed not only trophies and bones of antelopes, but also hippos' teeth hidden in a hut belonging to my neighbor's staff. Although the day before, the suspects had told my man that they were target shooting, now they told the police they had been chasing hippopotamus away. Since hippos don't come out during the daytime on the land around here, the men were obviously lying. They had been trusted with a shotgun and a few dogs to defend the place during the owner's absence, but as they had misused both, the gun and license were confiscated.

For two more days Coli and his mother remained at the scene of the tragedy. Whenever I approached they tried to hide, but they could not conceal their tails, so I always knew where they were. I was very relieved when they moved near the house.

Coli had grown considerably. I was also struck by how much older his mother's face had become and by the deep furrows she had around her nose. It was heartbreaking to see her gazing into space while clasping little Coli, who buried his head between her chin and her knees. Their bearing expressed their sorrow.

Two weeks later I heard the mother calling; she roared far longer than she ever had before. Was she communicating with a group of Colobus who sometimes came to the lake in the dry season, or was she teaching Coli how to roar? I never found out the answer, but from then on she called quite frequently, always starting with a smacking sound and then repeating the single roars.

Gradually the two began to play again. It was Coli who took the initiative. He pulled at his mother's tail until she could ignore him no longer; turning around she made him jump away, only to have her tail grabbed again. At siesta time she lay down and he would hop up and down on her until she sent him flying. This he considered a part of the game, and he would wait to repeat his performance until she had herself stretched out once more. I admired the patience with which she tolerated her indefatigable imp.

In mid-September I had to go for a month to the United States. When I told friends there of the Colobus tragedy, they suggested replacing the father by a captive male. Of course I was touched, but I did not accept their offer because I was not sure that my two would welcome a stranger into their territory. They might fight him or themselves clear out. Also, the imported male might not adapt to the new environment or be willing to take over a family.

When I got home I found the monkeys fit. Coli was now almost as large as his mother and had developed the bonnet so typical of the guerezas. He had invented a new game by letting himself fall with outstretched arms and legs into a thicket far below. He repeated this so often that I got worried, as he could not know whether the branches would support his weight or whether he might land on thorns and injure himself. He often fed on several trees far from his mother, but when sleeping he always buried himself in her arms.

One day I watched the seated pair spanking each other until the mother grabbed Coli's hand and held it close to his face, thus stopping him from hitting her again. Next day they disappeared. I next found them at the place the male had been shot. They remained there for two days and then vanished for four, after which Coli turned up alone at the house, very nervous and hiding himself whenever I came near. For the next three days he kept close and seemed increasingly frightened. Meanwhile, I searched for the female and found her on my neighbor's grounds, high up a tree. She did not seem surprised to see me and kept on feeding, in spite of the presence of many members of my staff. They told me that Coli had been spanking his mother so hard that she had got frightened and fled. In spite of my repeated calls to her, she did not move and stayed there for two days. When finally she reappeared near the house she edged herself cautiously near to Coli, though it took an hour before she had covered the 200 yards that separated them. Coli had watched her all the time but did not go to meet her. However, when they met there was a lot of hugging, nosing, and grooming before they started feeding.

The more independent Coli became, the more inquisitive he grew. In the very early morning I sometimes saw him venturing onto the ground. Looking carefully around to see if all was safe, he hopped about, chasing his tail, and he seemed pleased to discover a solid, flat base for this new game. Once I also saw his mother on the lawn, but only for a few moments. I laid out carrots, but they were ignored.

Coli often chewed sticks, and I wondered if that

might be due to changing his teeth. He was one year and ten months old.

On April 26, 1972, I was phoned by a farmer from the nearby hills who offered me a baby Colobus that he had found abandoned. Its mother had probably been killed by dogs when she was raiding vegetables. The farmer and I hoped that at such an early age the baby would be adopted by my Colobus, but I decided to keep the youngster confined until I could be sure that a happy relationship was developing.

A friend accompanied me when I went to collect the baby, so that I could look after the little one on the way home, across the sixty-odd miles of bad roads. En route we bought a feeding bottle, glucose, Farex, milk of magnesia (in case of stomach upset), and a crate of Nestlé's Ideal milk.

The farmer's daughter had been looking after the little monkey; when she came to greet us, he peeped at us from beneath her cardigan, staring at us with his large, expressive eyes. Judging by his coloring he was about two and a half months old.

When the girl handed him to me, he clung desperately to her woolen cardigan; only with great hesitation did he accept my blouse. He also refused to feed from the new bottle, so I had to borrow the old one. I was told that the baby had taken very quickly to bottle feeding. Every two hours he drank Ideal milk diluted with two-thirds water mixed with a little glucose, a diet I had recommended over the telephone to the farmer. In his droppings there were remains of fiber, which indicated that he had already eaten leaves.

To soften his hard belly, we took him into the garden, which was on a steep slope, for a little exercise. Having been released at the top end, the baby hopped downhill. I had to be quick to prevent him from disappearing into the forest undergrowth. When, later, I again let him go from the top end of the garden, he repeated the performance and made for the forest that had been his home.

Next I placed him near a bush in the open. He attempted to climb into the branches, but he needed someone to boost his bottom.

During our drive home the monkey chose my head as a lookout post and eagerly watched all that went on along the road. When he got tired, I wrapped him inside a towel to keep him in darkness and he instantly fell asleep. Shortly before reaching home he was sick, which I put down to the excitement of the day and to the rough drive.

When we arrived at Elsamere it was dusk. The monkey uttered his wee cry and duly did his job on the lawn. Though he had only given a faint sound, it was loud enough to bring Coli and his mother racing across the treetops. The mother stopped some fifteen feet above us, opening and closing her mouth repeatedly while staring at the baby. I had never known her to behave as she did now; I assumed she was showing friendliness. The baby was equally excited and responded by calling and trying to move toward her. But since it was too dark by now to let him go, I kept him on my lap while having a sundowner.

As time passed, the little monkey, in response to the agitation shown by our monkeys, became more and more restless, so I put him into a spacious wire crate. This I placed near my bed. When I retired the little Colobus found a cozy place around my neck, and from then onward he used the wire crate only to do his jobs in.

He had the softest fur, and when he touched my face with his tiny hands it was like being stroked with velvet.

I fed the baby three times before midnight. He always gave a warning when he needed the crate. Afterward he slept until dawn. During the night I was awakened by a clatter on the bedroom veranda, where I had left the remains of the sundowner.

In the early morning we heard Coli's mother calling very close, and the baby reacted instantly. I now found the plate and glass broken on the veranda floor. There were no footmarks by which I could trace the culprit. As I could not remember any of the wild animals ever having come onto the veranda, I assumed that it must have been the mother monkey frantic to get at the baby. This was extraordinary, since she was not nocturnal; also, she must have covered quite a long stretch of lawn and jumped onto the table.

In spite of her strange behavior, I was not yet sure if it was safe to let her have the little monkey. To gain time, I took him to the wired compound that my husband, George, had used for his injured lion. This was some distance from the house; here the baby could move about and get exercise. I helped him onto the lower branches of a senecio climber, hoping that he might eat the leaves, but he showed no interest. I then placed him on a pepper tree, but this, too, was not a success. At last I put him near the roots of an acacia; these he enjoyed exploring, and he also nibbled at the bark. Finally we sat on the lawn near the house, where I took photographs while the little monkey climbed across my legs and chewed at my rubber soles. He had very silky, curly hair on his head, back, and tail—which was much longer than his body. Under each of his nails (they were long and looked more like claws), he had a tiny ball—presumably these were adhesive suckers, for climbing. His teeth were well developed, though at this age he had only two incisors between the canines. I had counted four on the father's jaw after he died. Suddenly the telephone rang. I placed the baby in the nearby crate and went to answer it.

A few moments later I heard a cry; rushing out, I saw the mother Colobus at the crate. She had stretched her hands through the wire, and the baby was holding on to them. As soon as she noticed me she hurried to a tree some fifteen yards away. From there she watched us, opening and shutting her mouth rapidly, as she had done when we arrived.

Torn between my impulses to let her have the baby and to play it safe by keeping him for another month while he still needed a mixed diet of milk and leaves, I decided to risk letting them stay together.

I thought that if I allowed Coli's mother to take over, she, with her love and care, might speed up the little monkey's acceptance of solid food and ensure that he could live wild again.

I opened the door of the cage; in a flash the baby was out and hopping at top speed toward his adopted mother. Calling all the time, she met him on the ground, clutched him to her chest, and raced up high into the tree with him. Instantly the baby stopped crying. But as I watched the two through my field glasses hugging and cuddling each other, I wondered whether I had made the right decision: Would the mother be able to keep the infant alive, even though she had no milk?

Coli had so far kept in the background. Now he seemed intrigued, and he edged himself slowly nearer his mother. I watched, fascinated by the way in which she kept Coli in his place by moving her head upward in his direction and appearing to shoo him off while simultaneously moving a few yards away. She repeated this whenever Coli came too near, until he took the hint and remained at a safe distance. I thought it touching that Coli, who up to now had been the center of his mother's life, showed no jealousy. She kept the orphan mostly in a suckling position, and when his head fell back and he cried, she quickly supported him. Whenever the baby explored a nearby branch, she watched him anxiously and grabbed him if he went too far. Once

I saw her reaching for acacia leaves, chewing them, then bending her head over the baby's mouth; she seemed to me to be feeding him with the pulp.

Unfortunately the rains were due—the first shower fell the next day. The mother protected the baby under her arms as she had done up to now with Coli. He followed the two all the time without interfering. Through my binoculars I saw that the baby was getting very thin. The only food he had had since losing his mother was Ideal milk mixed with a little Farex.

To relieve my anxiety, my African staff assured me that sometimes their women, when they adopted a baby, produced a little milk, after a few days, provided that they had previously had a child. Doubting this, I telephoned a vet who confirmed my fears. It was a year and half since Coli's mother had weaned him, and her milk must have dried up.

During the night there was another storm, and I was very worried about the baby. I became even more so when the guard told me that the monkey had cried through the night.

As soon as the sun came out all three monkeys appeared on a low tree to warm themselves. The baby moved around the female while she fed, then she tried again to nurse him. Whenever his head fell back and he started crying, she instantly supported him and on a few occasions put some leaves into his wide-open mouth. This behavior was repeated in the intervals between three more cloudbursts. At tea time the monkeys settled near the forest on an acacia that was half covered with senecio. They were so low that I could easily watch the baby bending a senecio stalk into his mouth and nibbling at the leaves. Despite this encouraging action, I was not reassured, for his spine looked like a dark line, as if the hair had worn off. I watched them until it became too dark and another storm approached.

After a heavy night's rain I heard the mother calling at early dawn. Taking a flashlight, I rushed to the tree where she had been the previous evening and found her alone, gazing at the ground. Searching through the very thick undergrowth intermingled with senecio, I failed to find the baby and called one of my staff to bring a ladder. As soon as he approached, the mother fled into the forest. Climbing halfway up the senecio-covered tree, I found the little monkey hanging head down in the thicket, only just alive. He was wet and terribly emaciated.

I put him on top of a hot-water bottle, fed him milk and glucose, and gave him some Abidec with an eyedropper. After an hour he revived and drank quite well, but he was still too weak to move anything except his hands. Every hour I gave him another drink and kept him on the hot-water bottle. He seemed to me to be recovering. He could even sit up, so I risked driving over to a neighbor who had often reared animals, to borrow some Terramycin. I took the baby with me; on the way he produced firm, dark droppings, which indicated that he had eaten something during the last few days. On our return he had another meal of milk and glucose, after which he produced more firm droppings. I kept him on my lap and stroked him, which he seemed to like. Clasping my fingers with his tiny hands, he even smiled. I felt so happy, hoping that I might have succeeded in snatching him from death. We went on playing for another hour, until his hands loosened their grip on my fingers and his breathing ceased.

For yet another half hour the eyes seemed so alive that I could not believe he was dead.

Looking at his pitifully emaciated body, I felt deep remorse. Only now did it occur to me that the leaves he had eaten at his birthplace were growing at 2,000 feet higher than those at Elsamere and would be of a different species from ours. He may not have been able to adjust himself to this change of diet, aggravated as it was by the sudden stopping of milk. The heavy, unexpected rains no doubt added to the strain, not to mention having lost his mother and being obliged to adapt himself to three different foster mothers within seven days.

This tragedy, which could so easily have been avoided, proved once more how little we know about wild animals and how important research into their behavior is if we want to save them.

The fact that Colobus are highly protected does not save them from being poached. Unfortunately, they can easily get caught when they are still stiff from the cold nights at altitudes of over 7,000 feet.

All that poachers have to do is shake them off the trees and kill them.

I thought it would be interesting to know whether captive-born Colobus could be adopted by wild ones; if so, a healthy survival number could be maintained.

It was with this in mind that on October 29, 1974, I rescued (with the help of the Game Department) two female Colobus orphans. I assumed they were about one year old. They had been illegally purchased and had been kept in captivity for about five months. During this time they had been fed on raw peas, carrots, beans, potatoes, apples, and bread.

My hope of getting the orphans adopted failed because our Verreaux's eagle owls swooped down at them as soon as they arrived. Thus until they could defend themselves against these large birds of prey, the little monkeys had to be confined inside a spacious enclosure near my bedroom; it had wire stretched across the top so that no predators could harass the inhabitants.

From the beginning the mother Colobus and Coli showed great interest in the newcomers. They sat on the wooden post of the enclosure, guarding the babies by day and by night, while trying to reach the little ones through the wire and uttering soft calls. The orphans responded in a very friendly way, which gave me hope that my experiment might be successful.

One of the babies was older, larger, and stronger than the other and had her tail tassel cut short below the last vertebra, while the other had a normal tassel. By this I could easily identify them from any distance.

My main task was to get Short-tail and Long-tail used to natural food from the forest so that they would be independent by the time I released them; but when I offered them the leaves that Coli and his mother liked the babies refused them. I then tried different plants and found that only the leaves of the acacia trees and of a hairy climber agreed with their digestion. Strangely enough, they were crazy about the morning glories I had planted outside the enclosure, though they were poisonous to other animals. I soon realized that it would take several weeks, if not months, before I could release the little ones.

Grooming plays a most important part in the lives of these monkeys, so if they were to be kept happy and fit, I had to do my best to be a substitute for their mothers. They were very clean little creatures, never fouling their sleeping hut or perches. I made a swing for them, and soon, hanging upside down from it, they could outdo any circus clown. Both had unlimited energy, chasing each other around and around and ending up in a mock fight. Short-tail was usually the leader and teased the life out of Long-tail, but once she had had enough Short-tail cuddled up to her playmate.

If playing is a sign of happiness in animals, these two were obviously no longer frustrated.

By mid-December Short-tail (then about one year and three months old) changed her teeth, first dropping her lower incisors. During this period she was very greedy and jealous of Long-tail, sometimes tearing a carrot out of her mouth. When I gave it back to its owner, Short-tail hit me angrily.

Both were extremely sensitive to sound and often listened, with head turned upward and wide-open mouth, to noises such as the hooting of owls or the call of a fish eagle. They were alert also to the presence of a black-tipped mongoose. Whenever one emerged from the forest onto the lawn, Short-tail raced to the perch nearest the mongoose and gave a short grunt or a clicking sound, trying to frighten the enemy away.

On January 1, 1976, I heard Short-tail, then one year and four months old, making a weak attempt to roar. Lately she had become very aggressive and I had to avoid her sharp nips, especially when feeding her. Constantly looking around for danger, she shoved the peas so rapidly into her mouth that most of them fell to the ground; when grabbing carrots, she ate only the tops and threw the remainder away. I told her to eat more slowly. She looked at me and threw the peas around at even greater speed. The more I laughed, the faster the peas flew. Long-tail, much slower and very good-natured, picked them up. Her temperament was the opposite of Short-tail's. She enjoyed her food and inspected it very carefully, and she nibbled each carrot to its end.

I could not understand Short-tail's increasingly

aggressive behavior. Perhaps she was feeling frustrated, especially when Coli and his mother kept away for a day.

On January 13, 1976, the adults, who were watching the orphans eat carrots, stretched out for their midday snooze. All was so still and peaceful that I had an impulse to release the little ones. I opened the door to freedom, and before I knew what had happened the monkeys were out and hopping around.

At this sight Coli and his mother came down from the tree and made a slow approach. Short-tail hopped some hundred yards in the opposite direction across the lawn and onto the bird feeder. She was followed by Long-tail. Puzzled, Coli and his mother clicked their alarm sound. A few moments later the young ones climbed up a tree at the forest's edge. The adults joined them for a short time, then all returned into the enclosure. Soon Coli and his mother jumped into the tree that overshadows the enclosure and rested halfway up, as if to wait for the babies to follow. This tree was connected by wires to the corner posts of the enclosure. Short-tail dangled upside down along the wires, trying to reach the thick stem of the tree. Then, cleverly, she heaved herself into a fork, where she stopped, waiting for Long-tail; she, being much more cautious, attempted the crossing of the wire three times before succeeding in making the fork. Meanwhile, the grownups shinned right to the top of the acacia and showed no sign of wishing to help the little ones.

While the monkeys had a rest I blocked one door of the enclosure with a wooden frame, leaving only a small hole for Long-tail and Short-tail to slip through—thus preventing Coli and his mother from getting in. This was important because I might have to feed the little ones until they could survive on food from the forest, and I didn't want the adults to develop the habit of raiding their carrots. It was also important that the adults should teach the babies to live in the trees, since this was their natural habitat. As soon as this restricted entrance was completed the little ones came down from the tree and inspected it carefully. They had no difficulty in wriggling through the tiny hole and started to eat as if their great adventure had been nothing unusual. Coli and his mother followed and seemed puzzled at being separated from the orphans. They hopped onto the top wire of the enclosure, where they remained until dark. I found it prudent to confine the babies for the night until they had become used to their freedom.

Next morning, when I fed her, Short-tail hit and bit me. As soon as Coli and his mother appeared I opened the door. Short-tail rushed instantly out and up to the top of the tree. Long-tail, with difficulty and only after several attempts, managed to get into the tree. The mother monkey watched but made no attempt to help her as she clambered up and settled close to Short-tail. Our monkeys chose a branch a few yards below the orphans, and all had a good feed on the acacia leaves. The adults remained beneath the little ones, as if ready to stand by in case one should fall. Later all four disappeared into the forest.

At eight o'clock the next morning the orphans hopped onto the roof of the house and from there shinned down the drain pipe to the lawn. Then they went into the enclosure and straight to the water bowl, where they sucked and sucked. Later they fed ravenously and emitted a bad smell. This is typical of Colobus and is due to their unusually large stomach. The young monkeys seemed very tired. When there was no more food they joined the adults on a pepper tree and continued feeding. Sometimes I saw them let themselves fall five to six yards, always landing safely in the foliage below.

Short-tail and Long-tail never cuddled up to the mother monkey. Indeed, they always moved away if she came too close.

One morning I saw them making for a tree that I knew to be poisonous (*Nicotiana glauca*). I tried to divert them, but Short-tail had already stuffed a few leaves into her mouth. Half an hour later she vomited and lay flat on her belly inside the enclosure. When the sun became too hot she dragged herself under a palm frond shelter and collapsed. Long-tail, who had been rushing after her, sat very close and watched her. I telephoned Paul Sayer, the vet who had helped us for many years, whenever one of our wild animals was ill. During the few hours it took him to arrive from Nairobi, Short-tail grew cold and never stirred. Paul diagnosed severe poisoning but refrained from sedating her, fearing that a sedative might only upset her more. Meanwhile, he manipulated her stomach. He advised me to keep her warm and to let him know the next morning how she was. So I made her a comfortable bed of straw and covered her with a towel. Long-tail sat almost on top of her and acted as a hot-water bottle. At seven o'clock that evening Short-tail sat up twice for a few moments. When I looked in at ten o'clock she was warm and breathing normally. Long-tail seemed touchingly concerned and never left her post.

Two days later Short-tail had recovered. During this time Coli's mother showed great concern. After this, Short-tail became really attached to me. All four now spent most of their time in the forest, but they made short visits to get a few carrots and peas. Whenever the adults wanted carrots, too, the little ones turned their bottoms toward them in an upright position to show their submission. But carrots alone did not satisfy the adults, and they nibbled the flowers and leaves of the bougainvillaeas I had planted to cover the roofs of the house and garage. All my efforts to stop them from ruining the plants were unsuccessful. The adults now came daily to the lawn, which was the last thing I wanted them to do, for in my absence someone might catch them. The four monkeys showed great interest in their reflection in the large glass sliding doors of the veranda and often jumped with such force at the imaginary intruders that I feared they might injure themselves. The young ones showed a predilection for resin, which they licked off trees.

After Short-tail and Long-tail had lived free for two months, the forest was invaded by ten baboons, who were obviously not getting enough food on the hills in the dry season and had therefore come foraging near to the lake. They ate all the young trees I had planted as well as the *Candelabra euphorbia* lining the entrance drive, and they broke the guttering of the house; but what I feared most was that they might harm the little monkeys. All our efforts to chase the baboons away failed. When they first appeared Long-tail and Short-tail raced to safety, but after a while they got used to one another and I sometimes saw the Colobus sitting on the same tree as the baboons.

When later two vervet monkeys showed up, the Colobus reacted in the same way. This confirmed the belief that Colobus are very tolerant of other species of monkeys, even within their territories.

It was exactly nine days less than five months since I had released Long-tail and Short-tail on January 13, 1976, when for the first time I saw Coli's mother holding her arms around both orphans, who were cuddling up to her. From now on they were fully accepted as part of the family, and the mother treated them exactly as she had treated Coli.

This adoption had taken a long time—seven months—but now I knew there was a way to prevent the extermination of these lovely monkeys.

At the beginning of January 1976, when Coli was five and a half years old, he matured; from then on his character changed. Until then he had been respectful to his mother, regarding her as his superior. But from this point on he was the leader of the family and they all had to submit to him. Whenever his mother wanted a carrot she submitted to me and took the carrot very gently from my hand, but Coli often jumped at me, trying to push the carrot bowl out of my fingers to get the largest ones. He had become aware of his superior strength and made good use of it; but he was also the protector of the three females, deciding in which direction they should move and always waiting behind until all were safe. Recently I had watched Coli mounting his mother, but I assumed this was only the sex play of puberty. She had become much tamer and often hopped onto my writing table when I was typing on the veranda. Long-tail was always very friendly, and also very ladylike! Short-tail, on the contrary, continued to be aggressive, even though by now she must have known that she was getting her fair share of food and that I was as fond of her as I was of Long-tail.

Until 1976 we all lived happily together. Then Penny, a two-month-old leopard cub, arrived at Elsamere. Even though I confined her to the wired-in enclosure, the monkeys cleared out at once, and it was some days before they realized that the leopardess could do them no harm; then they cautiously returned. After this they teased her unmercifully through the wire while she tried to catch their tails.

I had waited several years to find a female leopard cub so that I could observe her behavior while rehabilitating her to her natural life, as I had done

35

with Elsa the lioness and Pippa the cheetah. In this way I would be able to complete my study of the three great cats of Africa. But to do this, I was going to have to move into the bush for an indefinite period. It was a great wrench to leave the monkeys, but I was lucky in finding tenants for Elsamere, the Aytons, who were animal lovers. They looked after the Colobus and continued to feed them carrots.

When Coli was seven and a half years old, I was delighted to receive a letter telling me that on January 29, 1978, Coli, Long-tail, and Short-tail had failed to come and fetch carrots and had spent all their time watching the mother give birth to a female baby. Next morning the mother came to collect a carrot, clutching the tiny white infant to her breast. From then on she remained high up in the trees while Coli protected his family fiercely, even growling at the camera below. When the baby was only two weeks old, she was able to hold onto her mother so that she could use her hands for climbing trees. At two months, although she was still suckling, she started to nibble carrots. By nineteen weeks she had acquired mature coloring and was independent of the mother, though she always remained close to her family.

At the beginning of June, friends needed a home for a year-old female Colobus called Gigi. Hoping that our monkeys might adopt her, they brought her to Elsamere. The Aytons kept her confined inside the boma to give all of the monkeys time to make friends.

When the excitement among our resident Colobus had abated, Gigi was accepted by all our family with the exception of Short-tail, who challenged her on every possible occasion. To make up for Short-tail's aggression, Long-tail tried to comfort Gigi through the wire; a bond developed between them.

It was unfortunate that during this time the Aytons had to leave Elsamere; new tenants moved in. Long-tail, being the most friendly and gentle, soon became their pet. They allowed their small child to feed her with candy, fruit, and tidbits. As Colobus are strictly leaf-eaters, Long-tail became ill and by October 13 was hardly able to move.

On October 15 Gigi's owners came to release Gigi from the boma. As soon as they opened the door she hopped out, followed by Short-tail, Long-tail, and Coli, who made clicking noises at her, frightening her. Gigi rushed to her friend Long-tail for protection, but in her panic she bowled her over. Before Long-tail, weak as she was, could pull herself together, Short-tail chased Gigi into the forest.

During the following two days Long-tail became too weak even to climb a tree. She finally disappeared and was never seen again.

Gigi was luckier: after surviving a few days in the forest, she found a new home a mile away, at a farm belonging to my neighbor, who fed her and treated her as a pet. Later, whenever I visited Elsamere—if only for a few hours—as soon as I called to them, the mother and her baby, Coli, and Short-tail came racing out of the forest to take carrots from my hand as though we had not been parted for fourteen months. Gigi appeared puzzled to see her family on such friendly terms with an apparent stranger and kept well out of reach, though her curiosity was such that she jumped as close to me as she dared, to look at me inquisitively with her large, expressive eyes.

When I felt the soft fingers of the Colobus touching my hands as trustingly as ever, I was overpowered with a happiness that was marred only by the absence of Long-tail, who had been my favorite.

Still, life had to go on. I tried to be grateful that the new baby was now filling the gap that poor Long-tail had left.

Verreaux's Eagle Owls

On our land at Elsamere, our home by Lake Naivasha in Kenya, was a little forest of acacia trees overshadowing a dense undergrowth of bush, climbers, and creepers. It provided shelter for reed and bushbuck, otters, marsh mongoose, civet, genets, antbears, duikers, dik-dik, and Colobus monkeys, as well as many birds. The most endearing of these were a pair of Verreaux's eagle owls who occupied an abandoned fish eagle nest—a large contraption of sticks about three feet across, set high up in a tree that partly overhung the lake.

The ornithologist Leslie Brown, who was commissioned by the Food and Agriculture Organization to do a count of all the birds on Lake Naivasha, had discovered it on one of his monthly cruises. When he first saw it, the female was incubating; six

41

days later he noticed a pure-white young bird in the nest.

After about three months I found the owlet half a mile from its nest in the forest not far from the house. By then its fluffy plumage had turned smoky gray; although it was almost as large as the parents, there was no sign of horns.

Verreaux's eagle owl (*Bubo lacteus*), the third largest owl in the world and the largest in Africa, is well known throughout Senegal, the Sudan, and Ethiopia, right down to South Africa; but little is known of the habits of these spectacular birds, which have a wingspan of twenty-three inches.

The mature birds are very striking. Their black eyes, the size of Ping-Pong balls, are protected by bright-pink eyelids fringed by white eyelashes. The hooked beak is as large as a lion's claw; it grows out from a fluffy mustache of feathers that are darker than those of the pale-gray face, which is framed by a black ring of fluff that forms a white beard below the beak. The large horns are lined with black feathers and are separated by a black-and-white speckled triangle which covers the forehead.

The owls' formidable talons can carry a bird up to the size of a chicken; they are in striking contrast to the white, fluffy leg covers that match a line of pure-white blobs on the dark-brown body. The birds range in height from twenty-four to twenty-six inches.

I loved watching these owls early in the morning as they perched high above my bedroom.

The youngest could not hoot as yet and only uttered a whistling sound when it was hungry. To whistle is *pfeifen* in German, so I named the young owl Pfeifer. It soon came sailing through the forest whenever I called it to give it food.

My feeding of the owls gradually developed while we were clearing the ground around the house of mole rats, which were most destructive to the lawn. The owls regarded these rodents as a great delicacy and gobbled two to three a day. Since those rats have a body length of some eight inches, they occasionally got stuck halfway down the owls' throats; the birds had to avoid choking by convulsive vomiting. When concentrating on this painful operation the owls closed their eyes, looking—with their bright-pink eyelids and half a rat sticking out from their beaks—ludicrous and pathetic. No matter how long it took to get the rat into the stomach, the feeding was followed by an elaborate cleaning of the beak, which was wiped on both sides of a branch until there was no trace of blood left.

In eagle owls and in many other species of owl, the male is smaller than the female. But it seemed unique to our family that the father should soon take over all maternal duties in regard to his offspring, Pfeifer, who—judging by her enormous size—was obviously a female. Whenever she hooted and did a hunger dance, swaying her body to and fro with lowered head, her father beak-fed her with small pieces of meat, a beetle, or whatever he could find, while her mother sat aloof high up in a tree.

43

When the grounds had been cleared of mole rats, I continued feeding the owls with raw meat to save the smaller birds around the place, which otherwise would have become their victims. I provided plenty of food, so it seemed odd that the mother never came for meat. Only once did I see her venture to the ground to catch a mole rat, which she carried off instantly to her tree. The father followed her and then sat opposite his mate, plucking her head for several minutes. There was no sign of fighting for the rat.

Pfeifer rarely accompanied her mother and spent most of her time with her father. When she was five months old, her horns developed and her color changed to light brown. She was by then much larger than her father; it seemed ridiculous for her still to perform her submission rites when begging for food, for by then she was capable of killing rodents and an occasional snake. Yet after doing so, she waited for her father to feed them to her. There are remarkably few snakes at Elsamere: those I saw were almost always dangling from the beak of an owl.

Normally, when landing, owls need a long landing strip; but when attacking snakes, they drop from short distances onto their victims and kill them instantly. Afterward the laborious swallowing process, to get the long reptile down in one piece, begins; often this takes half an hour.

Pfeifer soon learned from her parents how to lie on the ground with widespread wings and remain completely motionless. This may have been partly to

Verreaux's eagle owl with mole rat

Pfeifer on tree trunk

Joy Adamson feeding an owl

Owl shamming death

Owl anting

John Cooper releases Bundu

sun herself or for "anting," but more often, I believe, it was to trick the smaller birds into coming within her reach. They were certainly intrigued by an apparently dead owl, and sometimes they ventured fatally close.

Verreaux's eagle owls can be very clever at shamming death, not only to deceive their prey but also to escape danger to themselves.

One day I was walking through the bush with a gunbearer, when I noticed stretched out in the grass a large owl who had badly injured one eye. Observing its powerful talons, I did not like the prospect of carrying the bird home, so I sent the gunbearer to the house to ask George to bring a strong piece of cloth and collect us in the Land Rover. While waiting, I sat near the owl, who seemed almost dead, though after a time she opened her one good eye. As soon as we heard the car she collapsed and remained apparently lifeless while we placed her in a burlap sack and drove home. On arrival she hung limp in my arms and did not react when we examined her. I decided that now she was really dead and placed her on the ground, ready for burial, but George suggested we should give a last test. He shot a pigeon, and we then put the two "dead" birds inside a wired compound. After an hour we returned to find the owl apparently as lifeless as before, though lying in a different position; of the pigeon there was no trace. George went off to shoot another pigeon; he placed it near the owl. This time, very cautiously, we hid ourselves close to the enclosure and surprised the owl enjoying her meal. When she noticed us she instantly fell "dead" again.

These faked-death performances became routine whenever a person approached her. Testing her self-control, I once sketched her while she hung upside down on the compound wire; this took a long time, but she never made a movement.

She had shammed herself into captivity, which was certainly to her advantage, for she could now recover safely from her injuries. After two months we released her.

Whenever I called Pfeifer for food, the father turned up with her and had the first helping. He ignored her submission dance, and she often had to beg a long time before she got her share.

One morning I found Pfeifer sitting on a rotten tree trunk that was overgrown with creepers. She had become entangled in the strong tendrils; the more she struggled, the more firmly she was caught. Finally she seemed unable to move, so I went to her rescue. I had never touched her before, but after I reached her, having climbed up the longest ladder we had, she sat quite still during my efforts to free her.

She was in every sense a wild owl. I had no intention of taming her, though gradually a bond developed between us and she seemed to trust me completely.

She showed this whenever I held out meat to her: she would walk slowly up to me in her typical sailor's gait, shifting her weight from one white, fluffy-booted leg to the other; then she would take her food to the lawn and eat it within a few inches of me. I was often tempted to put my hands into her soft plumage, but I should never have forgiven myself if by doing this, I might have tamed her to the point where other human beings might become a danger to her.

Pfeifer trusted me, and to get a mouse she sometimes even ventured onto the veranda floor while I was having breakfast, but she never allowed visitors to come near her.

When she was fourteen months old, her coloring was that of a mature bird. About this time her father became rather aloof; he not only stopped feeding Pfeifer, but often took his food deep into the forest. I wondered if he was feeding his mate, who had been absent for a few weeks.

One day my neighbors' dogs killed a genet, a catlike animal. Hearing their barks, I rushed to the scene, hoping to rescue the genet, but I arrived too late, so I took the carcass. After cutting it into small sections, I offered it to the owls.

Pfeifer came; after walking around and around the tail, she finally decided against it. The genet certainly had an extremely strong odor, which was repulsive not only to me but evidently also to the birds, for as soon as Pfeifer left a flock of starlings descended. They were always on the lookout for any greasy meal and waited daily for their share of bacon rinds and cheese. Now they examined the remains of the genet very cautiously, but none went close

47

enough even to peck at it. They reacted in the same way to a puff adder I had killed.

I have never been able to understand where owls draw the line about eating carrion. Ours feasted on the mole rats we supplied them with, though the rodents were often quite stiff by the time we retrieved them from the traps. But birds that had killed themselves by flying into the windows the owls found as unpalatable as they did the puff adder and the genet.

I was surprised when I saw Pfeifer eating a dead fish that had been dropped by a fish eagle. I knew that the fish eagles often tried to steal the meat I had laid out for the owls, but I had never seen the owls catching fish or even flying near the lake to drink. They, like the Colobus monkeys, appeared to get all the liquid they needed from their solid food.

Now, in mid-November, Pfeifer was one and half years old. Her mother had been missing for a few weeks, so I was relieved to see her once again with her mate. They sat for a long time holding their heads close together and rubbing beaks.

A few days later I was just in time to see the mother fly from a tree onto the ground, followed by the male, who watched her pick up a green snake and take it to the tree. I fetched the movie camera and filmed her disentangling the snake from her talons and swallowing it; but soon she pulled it out again with her talons, and after first tackling the intestines, swallowed the rest. All this took five minutes. From now on, the mother appeared regularly for food, something she had never done before.

The male now started to watch my movements when I was about to feed the birds, so as to make sure that he always got in first. When he had fed he would then smack his beak, thus calling Pfeifer and her mother, who answered from the forest with their typical hunger screech. As soon as they appeared, the male fed both of them. I watched this for the last time on March 24, 1972, before leaving on a safari. When I returned on April 17 the father and mother owl were missing.

I set out to search for them and found the pair less than a mile outside my boundary. The female was incubating on an abandoned fish eagle nest. She had chosen the tallest acacia from among a patch of trees close to the road that leads around the lake. During the next few days I visited the place frequently. On a few occasions I saw only one owl and assumed the other was out hunting. Without her parents Pfeifer seemed to be very lonely; far more often than before, she took her meat from within a few inches of me.

I had to go away again from May 7 to 25. On my return late one afternoon Pfeifer came sailing along and gave me a hooting welcome. She arrived from the direction of the new nest, where I found her mother still incubating. From now on in the mornings and late afternoons Pfeifer always took the meat straight to her parents. Often she made three or four trips, and I was fascinated to see that she always carried off the biggest piece. It may be that she did this to save an extra journey; certainly she fed the others before herself. Unfortunately her errands were soon noticed by the fish eagles, who kept an all-day watch on her movements. Once I saw two of them attacking her. She had no chance of saving the meat, though she defended it with her beak and wings as well as she could. After this she was very cautious and made sure that no fish eagle was in sight before she started on her feeding mission. Sometimes she came back quickly and followed me around, uttering her hunger screech until I gave her more meat, which she took to the nest.

On June 7 I saw the mother owl still incubating. Counting the days since the pair had been missing from Elsamere, I calculated that she had been on the nest for fifty-two days. Normally the incubation period lasts only twenty-five days.

Again I had to go away. On my return, hardly had I stopped the car when Pfeifer appeared, screeching for food. While the cook prepared it I walked over to the nest and found the parents sitting on a tree next to the one on which the nest was. I noticed some white fluff just visible above its rim; it proved to be the head of a new chick. A few moments later Pfeifer flew in and fed the owlet. The parents watched without stirring. I observed that the mother had lost most of her tail feathers during her long period of incubation on the rough nest. I thought the chick must now be about three weeks old. It was as large as a chicken and was almost white. On my way back to the house Pfeifer followed me, obviously wanting more meat. Of the two pieces I gave her, she ate one and carried the other to the nest.

Next day the male was absent; Pfeifer fed the owlet in the morning and called loudly at tea time, demanding more food. I went to the nest and found the mother sitting within six feet of the chick, which was visible up to its shoulders. The mother called all the time and was answered by Pfeifer as she came along, resting on several trees during the long flight. At her last stop, her mother flew to meet her, grabbed the meat, and ate it. Followed by Pfeifer, I returned to the house to get another ration for the owlet. From now on, because of the fish eagles, we often shared the feeding missions. They knew Pfeifer's resting trees and frequently ambushed her from them. One norning I saw her collide with one of the raiders in mid-air. After losing a few feathers, she reached a tree, only to be attacked again. While dangling upside down by one foot from a branch, she held her load with the other, bravely defending it until the fish eagle left, defeated. Although her life was often in danger during those flights, she flew, undeterred, every morning and afternoon to feed her rival. I say "rival" because I feared that sooner or later the new owlet would take over Pfeifer's place and force her to find a new territory. Meanwhile, she played a vital role in feeding the owlet so that the mother could keep guard all day—not only to protect it from the fish eagles but also from two Augur buzzards who often cruised around the nest.

The father's role was dubious; he sometimes kept away for weeks, leaving the catering to Pfeifer and me. On these occasions I carried meat to the mother, dropping it right under her tree and guarding it from fish eagles until she had taken it. It was interesting that Pfeifer helped with the feeding only when the father was away; as soon as he reappeared, she did not venture near the nest. Each of the owls had a distinct hoot that I could recognize.

When the chick was about one month old it turned silver gray, while its face remained white. There was no sign yet of a black ring or of pink eyelids, though it had developed some fluff where later the horns would be. It was extremely difficult to make a photographic record of the chick because the tree was so high. If I wanted to get a view of what was going on inside the nest I had to keep such a long way away that even with a 400 millimeter telescopic lens the pictures were not satisfactory.

On July 30 I was awakened by a great din. We hurried to the nest, where I found the mother owl sitting at the far end of the tree within six feet of another bird. At first I believed it to be Pfeifer, but when I looked through the binoculars I recognized the chick by its white face and silver-gray, fluffy plumage, with its wing feathers turning to light brown. It balanced itself clumsily with outstretched wings. If this chick had, as we believed, hatched on

June 9, it had left its nest for the first time within seven and a half weeks.

Next morning I was awakened at six o'clock by the mother's hunger screech. She was extremely nervous and did not come close to collect the meat.

The following morning the mother called again at six. After feeding her we went to the nest, where I saw the chick and Pfeifer at the far end of the tree. Later I placed three large lumps of meat under it; Pfeifer picked up one and took it to the chick. As the owlet had difficulty in tearing it to pieces, Pfeifer pulped it and waited patiently for half an hour until the owlet had eaten all of it. She then repeated this operation with the two remaining lumps.

The morning after, Pfeifer called at Elsamere, while the mother sat with the owlet outside the nest. She collected one of the pieces of the meat I had brought and took it to a tree some distance away. There she was attacked by an Augur buzzard. She snapped her bill at him. She lost a few feathers in the encounter but managed to save the meat and to fly nearer to the chick, though she was again attacked on her way. Finally she defeated the Augur and landed in the nest. From there she called the chick, which staggered awkwardly along the branch. But moving along a smooth branch was easy compared to climbing onto a bulky nest that had sticks protruding in every direction. Struggling to get into this spiky fortress, the chick was defeated. The mother, who was now calling with a soft sound I had never heard before, had entered the nest and was dangling the meat over the rim, obviously trying to encourage her young to greater effort. When she realized the chick could not make it, she clambered down to it, and, while feeding it, she retreated slowly into the nest, the little one following stick by stick until both disappeared inside. As soon as the owlet was safely settled the mother collected the second lump of meat and flew to the tree where the Augur had attacked her. By the way she now gulped down the meat, I could judge how hungry she must have been.

Pfeifer was on duty next morning guarding the chick. As soon as I dropped some meat she swooped down and secured the biggest piece in her talons. Then she sat for a long time staring at me. A friend tried to take a picture of the two of us but came too close for Pfeifer's liking: hooting in alarm, she flew off and landed on the nest, where she called in the soft tone that her mother had used the day before. The chick had great difficulty in leaving its precarious position, so after waiting for some twenty minutes, Pfeifer brought the meat to it and beak-fed it. She herself could easily have eaten the meat during this time, but she waited until the chick was satisfied and only then parachuted to the ground and got a piece for herself. I had now for the first time a full view of the chick and saw that its tail coverts, primary feathers, mantle, and rump were pale brown, while the rest of its body was covered with smoky-gray down.

When we returned in the afternoon, Pfeifer had left and the mother was guarding the chick. I had brought two small pieces of meat and one large one; the mother ate the small ones. After storing the large piece in the crotch of a neighboring tree, she settled within a yard of the nest for her snooze. I had been puzzled by the recent shift of duties between the mother and Pfeifer; I was even more surprised when, the next morning, the father turned up and remained with Pfeifer at Elsamere while the mother cared for the chick.

On the afternoon of August 5 we arrived just in time to see the father mating Pfeifer. Although it was already getting dark, we watched the mounting clearly; it lasted about half a minute. Of course we could not know whether Pfeifer had conceived. She was two years and two months old. Next morning Pfeifer was again with her father at Elsamere, while the mother spent all day with the chick, which was by now well able to fly a few yards.

About this time I had to go on a safari, so I was absent for twenty days. As I had no means of keeping track of the owls, I feared that I might lose them, particularly as the tree on which the chick had its first outing was nearer to my neighbor's property than to our house. My relief was therefore great when on my return I found the chick near its old home and the good Pfeifer looking after it. On the day of my arrival she had a fierce clash with a fish eagle. They thrashed their wings against each other and somersaulted in the air; finally Pfeifer won. All

55

the owls were fit and seemed to have accepted the new chick within their territory. Its back was now covered with buff down, but it still had no horns. As if to make up for this, it had the biggest eyes I had ever seen any owl to have, and it was much larger than its mother. I believed it to be a female and named her Bundu (which means owl in Kiswahili). She seemed to be more at home on the ground than in the trees. One morning I found her having a shower under the water sprinkler; I had never known any other owls do this.

Up to now, Bundu had always followed Pfeifer or her mother at feeding time, and after submitting with her hunger dance and whistling screech, had been fed by them. Now she was about four months old, and Pfeifer seemed to think that it was time for her to learn how to fend for herself. So when her most appealing hunger dances were ignored, or, even worse, when Pfeifer went on eating all the food to the last morsel and pecking at her if she attempted to join in, Bundu began to spend her mornings searching for beetles or insects in the grass. She also seemed intrigued by all the smaller birds, but she was not yet able to catch them. Meanwhile, Pfeifer watched to make sure that Bundu learned her lessons.

At four months Bundu's eyelids had turned pale pink, which enhanced her beauty. Like all young animals I have known intimately, her eyes still had a soft, trusting expression very different from the hard glance of adult wild animals, who know the dangers life has in store for them.

I now stopped feeding the owls on lean meat and instead offered them chicken heads, which I was given by a nearby poultry farmer. The owls preferred this diet, which was more natural to them and provided them with more calcium. They swallowed the head in one gulp, feathers, beak, bones, and all, and managed to eat as many as ten a day.

When Bundu was six months old I spotted her deep in the foliage of a pepper tree near the lake, clashing wings with Pfeifer. A few moments later she was on the lawn and struggling up one of the logs I had placed along the lake front to keep the hippos away; she flapped her large wings, got entangled in the weed, and finally hung upside down, unable to move. I came to her rescue and freed her, but instead of flying up the tree into safety, she hopped off into even denser undergrowth. This was such a strange reaction that I suspected something must be wrong. Later she clambered clumsily from branch to branch into a thicket halfway up a pepper tree, where she was almost invisible. She remained there until after dark. This odd behavior confirmed my suspicions.

Early next morning I saw Pfeifer on the pepper tree within a few yards of the place where I had last seen the young owl. She was looking intently into the undergrowth below. Assuming that Bundu must be there, I crept through a mass of knee-high nettles, fallen bushes, and lianas; I screened every inch but found no trace of her. Still, Pfeifer kept on looking at the same spot. The parents, too, had turned up, but they seemed unconcerned and spent the whole day asleep on their favorite tree.

By now I was alarmed, fearing that Bundu had become a victim of the local otters or of the genets who often came onto the lawn after dark. Luckily, on the following afternoon I discovered her hidden in the pepper tree. She was very hungry: when she saw me she straight away started her hunger dance and clambered carefully along the branches to the ground. I brought her a few chicken heads, and she allowed me to place them at her feet, which she never had before. Obviously she did not want to fly, for she kept on walking. I followed slowly until she stopped, and I sat within a few inches of her and stroked her. This was the first time I touched her, and I only did so to find out whether she was injured. As I stroked her gently, I noticed that she reacted when I touched her right wing, so I decided to take her to the large outdoor enclosure. This was completely wired in, including the top, and made an ideal aviary. Here Bundu would be safe from predators and I could keep her under observation until I got a vet to examine her. Watching her powerful talons and beak, I approached her slowly from the rear and grabbed her quickly. She kicked her talons into my abdomen piercing my corduroys and leaving me with bleeding punctures. As soon as she was safely inside the enclosure, I put a few long bamboo poles up for her to perch on, nailed wooden boards across the corners for her to feed on, and put up a small triangular ladder for her to climb. Finally I placed a large wooden hut in the center as a shelter. The compound was next to my bedroom, so if Bundu was in danger during the night I would hear her slightest sound. She settled down immediately, no doubt because she was in familiar surroundings and could see her family perching on the nearby trees.

Next morning Pfeifer took up her position on a corner post of the enclosure, evidently puzzled at being separated by wire from Bundu. The owlet seemed so much better that I felt guilty at having locked her up, and so, since Pfeifer was close by, I decided to release her and see if she could fly across a greater distance than the enclosure provided. Wrapping a towel over her, I carried her outside. Pfeifer watched this eagerly and soon joined Bundu, who walked with her sailor's gait across the lawn for about a hundred yards, making straight for the forest. It was plain that she could not fly, so I hurried after her and reached her just as she tried to hide under a fallen tree, where she would have been out of sight. I then returned her to the enclosure. During all the next day Bundu snapped her bill whenever I approached her; then at last she accepted me again as a friend.

I tried to contact John Cooper, a vet who specializes in birds—in particular, in birds of prey. Before coming to Kenya, he worked in England, where he had made a study of the diseases and treatment of captive and wild birds of prey. He also had experience in the rehabilitation of such birds, including owls. At this time he was attached to the Veterinary Department in Nairobi. When I described Bundu's case to him he came immediately. The bird, faced with a stranger, promptly shammed death and thus saved herself from being anesthetized for the ensuing examination. She remained quite still while John Cooper diagnosed a break of the ulna and radius of her right wing, which he estimated had happened about two and a half weeks previously. He took samples of blood, of excrement, and of pellets. He then injected her with a vitamin-mineral preparation and gave her calcium tablets by mouth. Finally he suggested a month's confinement, during which time she was to be fed on white (laboratory) mice—which are rich in bone-forming minerals, especially calcium; he offered to send me a supply twice a week. Before he left he clipped Bundu's talons, both to reduce the damage she might do me and to keep her from injuring her own feet if the talons should become sharp and overgrown. He also cleaned her soiled tail and wing feathers. He identified her tentatively as a female.

I very much admired the great gentleness with which he handled this powerful bird, and by the time he left I felt I had made a new friend.

Feeding Bundu was no easy job, for although she was now seven months old and could kill small mice and lizards, she still kept to her instinctive sub-

mission gesture before eating. It appeared that I was cast in the role of her mother or of Pfeifer. Placing a dead mouse near Bundu's perch would not do: I had to dangle it in front of her beak for her to inspect it from every angle before she would grip it, transfer it to her talons, and squeeze it hard. If I dared touch her during this killing rite, she pecked savagely; even after these lengthy performances she often dropped the mouse to the ground to make me pick it up and repeat the dangling process.

The mice provided all the guts, pelts, bones, and meat needed to counteract Bundu's calcium deficiency. However, she had become so used to the lean meat I had previously given her that a contest developed between us, for she dropped the mice until I gave her the lean meat, and the only alternative was to starve her until she consented to eat the mouse. It often took me more than an hour to get her to swallow any food, so I was lucky when I succeeded in feeding her several mice in a day. She usually ate in the early mornings and at dusk. Although she slept most of the day, she seemed to need company, so I did my typing next to her and sometimes sketched her. I had lost the use of my right hand as a result of a car accident, but having such a perfect model, I could not resist painting Bundu, however difficult it was to hold a brush.

During the midday heat the owl panted heavily; she seemed to find relief by stretching herself as high as she could, thus appearing almost twice as tall and half as wide as usual. Keeping her bill wide

open and closing her pink eyelids, she puffed her throat up in rapid spasms for several minutes. When she had completed these cooling activities she was ready to be fed.

I was fascinated to discover that she did not recognize me when I wore unfamiliar clothing. I had observed the same with Elsa's and Pippa's families and had heard of other wild animals reacting in this way. Knowing that owls are among the nocturnal predators with the best eyesight, I was puzzled that they should seem to depend more on colors than on features for visual recognition.

John Cooper came often to check Bundu's recovery. We were anxious to release her as soon as possible so that she would not become too dependent on me; also she had recently developed a running nose, and she had a bald patch above her beak, which, in spite of the ointment with which it was treated, grew larger every day. Both were signs of stress. Since she was still in a transitional stage, being able to feed herself but still needing to make submission to her mother before eating, I was concerned to keep Pfeifer nearby to take over from me when Bundu was released.

To achieve this, I fed Pfeifer when I fed Bundu; this inevitably attracted the fish eagles. They besieged the place and perched on the trees above the compound, sitting on the same branch as the Colobus monkeys, who had taken a great interest in Bundu ever since she had arrived at Elsamere. But while the monkeys were accepted by the owls as

harmless friends and vice versa, the fish eagles were dangerous rivals, and they often attacked Pfeifer. I wondered how much longer she would put up with them in order to remain close to Bundu. If she were to abandon her now, I would have to tame the owl, as she would be unable to survive on her own. Fortunately Pfeifer continued her vigil until, after five and a half weeks, Bundu's fractures had healed, her condition had improved, and she was able to be released.

On January 22, 1973, John Cooper came to help with this operation. After a last check-up, during which Bundu faked death, he force-fed her two mice so that she would start her flight to freedom with a full stomach; then, under the tree from which Pfeifer and the mother had been watching us, he threw her into space. Instantly she opened her wings, and after a perfect flight she landed on a tree some hundred yards away. It was thrilling to see her taking off so effortlessly. At first she settled down, but it was not long before the Colobus monkeys stirred her into action. They, too, had been watching us since lunchtime, when we started the release, and now they raced up to Bundu, apparently happy to see her in her natural world again. Coli in particular appeared overjoyed. He jumped around Bundu and would not leave her alone until she walked to the far end of the branch and into thick foliage where he could not follow her.

Pfeifer and her mother flew in at dusk. I had left meat for the owls on the lawn; Pfeifer collected a piece and took it to Bundu. To my amazement, her mother instantly attacked Bundu, who fell off the branch into some thorny foliage. She hung there upside down for three or four minutes before she was able to free herself. Then she flew a few hundred yards into the forest, her mother following close to her and Pfeifer a little behind. Pfeifer still had some of the meat in her beak and settled with this on a branch. A few moments later Bundu emerged from the undergrowth and landed next to Pfeifer. By then it was too dark to follow what went on, but at least I knew that Bundu was not alone. Later Pfeifer hooted her hunger screech near the house, and after I had given her more meat she flew off with it in Bundu's direction. I was puzzled that the mother had attacked Bundu; perhaps she had done this for educational reasons, wanting to force the owl to hunt for herself, but, since she had previously left most of the feeding to Pfeifer, I could not understand her behavior. If she took a dislike to Bundu she would be much more dangerous to her than the fish eagles were.

Next morning I found Bundu still in the same area, but Pfeifer and the mother had moved nearer to the house and remained there all day. At dusk the owlet flew close to Pfeifer, who soon brought her some meat I had left on the ground. A little later Bundu flew off, and by the time Pfeifer left it was dark. Unfortunately, in the dark, the eyes of Verreaux's eagle owls do not reflect a flashlight, so unless they made a noise, it was extremely difficult to spot them.

Two days later I was awakened at two in the morning by Bundu's hunger screech. There she was, sitting on the lawn, obviously very hungry. Pfeifer was also close by, but both flew off as soon as I focused the beam of the spotlight on them. I left some meat out.

Next morning the mother bird sat on a tree near the scene with a piece of meat in her talons. Close to her was Pfeifer, who was scratching Bundu's head with her beak. A little farther along on a branch of the same acacia tree, the Colobus were munching leaves. Later in the afternoon the father owl turned up and settled on the same tree. I had provided food on the ground right underneath them; I was surprised when I saw Bundu flying down to eat one chicken head and then carry another into a tree. The mother and Pfeifer watched this but kept still; later Pfeifer followed Bundu. By then it was too dark to see what happened, but at least I had seen Bundu for the first time eating independently in view of her family.

Next day all the owls had disappeared into the forest, from where I heard their hoots. When they returned Bundu settled away from her family on a tree that overshadowed my little vegetable garden, which was fenced in with wire of much smaller mesh than the one around the compound intended to keep the antelopes out. I left a good supply of food for her. Not only did she take advantage of this safe feeding place, but so did the rest of her family. Never again did I see them feeding her.

Word of my free table must have gone around among the wild creatures, for I saw the shapes of various animals coming in increasing numbers after dark to the fleshpots I provided. About this time George came to Elsamere for a few days; enchanted by our nocturnal visitors, he installed an electric light on a tree to illuminate the lawn near the veranda so that we could have a better view of our night population.

A genet was among those who appeared; she was graceful and attractive, with spots and stripes on light-gold fur. She usually came rather late, except for one evening when she broke all the rules of feeding priorities. I was watching Bundu gobble up five chicken heads, when suddenly the genet sneaked up from behind. I was terrified that she might kill the owl, who, unaware of her presence, was enjoying her meal. Before I could intervene the genet rushed at Bundu, who, hopping off the ground with her meat, let the genet pass right under her and then descended and continued feeding. A moment later the genet repeated her charge; Bundu hopped up again with the meat in her talons, letting the genet once more pass beneath her. This obviously infuriated the genet, who, swinging around like lightning, attacked for a third time, only to be defeated by another hop. By then Bundu had had enough, and, spreading out her wings to their full length, she charged the genet, who bolted. After this the owl went on with her meal as if the genet had never existed. I had watched this encounter with great anxiety, hoping that the genet did not know that Bundu was mostly feathers and that if she had jumped at her neck, she could have killed her easily.

When I told this story to Leslie Brown he was not much impressed, for he had witnessed a Verreaux's eagle owl's encounter with a rhino that ran away as soon as the owl had put on her bluffing act.

These days Bundu kept to herself, usually in the pepper tree close to the lake. Perhaps, in its dense foliage, she felt safe from fish eagles; also, since it was a favorite resting place for the Colobus, she may have felt doubly protected.

At dusk eighteen days after her release I placed eight chicken heads below the pepper tree. She looked at them intensely but kept aloof on her high perch. About two hours later I heard her hunger screech and found her sitting opposite Pfeifer on a tree illuminated by the lamp. Pfeifer was eating a chicken head, completely unconcerned, while Bundu swayed to and fro with wings widespread, begging for food. She continued her hunger dance for some ten minutes but was ignored. I switched off the light in case it was upsetting the birds, but this had no effect. Long after I retired I heard Bundu still screeching. She took no meat the next morning and kept away from the other owls, changing position frequently, until finally she settled with Pfeifer; soon they were preening each other's heads, while their mother dozed some three yards away and their father a little farther off. Bundu then tried to join her father but got such a rebuff that she hurried back to Pfeifer; both came down to the meat, and they fed side by side. I could not understand Bundu's sudden relapse into submission, as she had fed independently for quite some time.

I was not worried when Pfeifer failed to appear on February 13. But when she went missing for two weeks, I became alarmed. We searched right up into the hills and looked at every tree along the lakeshore but could find no trace of her. Another two weeks passed without a sighting. My servants bought their food three miles from Elsamere, at a small shop that stands on private land near a patch of tall acacia trees. On two of these were abandoned fish eagle nests; near them my man saw Pfeifer.

I went there instantly and found her in the company of another owl close to one of the nests. I could not make out the sex of her companion or see whether the two had occupied the nest. I went there every few days, but I did not see Pfeifer again. Obviously she was looking for a new territory; my fear, when Bundu was a nestling, that Pfeifer might have to give way to her had proved justified. I could only hope that our relationship had not impaired Pfeifer's wild instincts and that she would soon hatch her own family.

Meanwhile, I tried to see that Bundu always got enough to eat. One evening I found her sitting half-submerged inside the birdbath that I had made in a little rock garden. Although it was pitch dark by then, she sat in the cool water for a long time. I could not understand her unusual behavior, since no owl had ever used the birdbath.

Bundu was now one year old and had developed into a very handsome bird. She still had the same soft and trusting expression, although she was able to cope with her occasional clash with a fish eagle. She seemed to trust me, but she lived the life of a wild Verreaux's eagle owl, and I was glad to know that the relationship that had developed while I was nursing her inside the compound had left no mark on her.

In early December Bundu had been alone at Elsamere for several months. I had fed her off and on and did so again after dark on December 10. Then, to my surprise, three owls came to the chicken heads, while a fourth, a smaller and shy one, remained at some distance. I was still more surprised when I recognized Pfeifer feeding next to Bundu.

When I had found Pfeifer in the acacia forest ten months earlier I had assumed that she had been driven away by the parents and had started her own family in a new territory. It seemed extraordinary that she would now return together with her chick. Or was it her mother's chick? Both had been away long enough to have incubated an egg.

The fact that Pfeifer had come back to her parents' territory made me believe that she was the mother of the shy owlet in the background. I was happy that she trusted me to help her feed her chick—I could almost hear her telling the other owls, "Let's take our chicks to Elsamere. That saves us a lot of work." When I approached to within two yards of her, she continued gulping down a chicken head as if I were not there.

Knowing that Bundu had been about three and a half months old before she could fly the distance from her nest to Elsamere, I reckoned that this new owlet was about the same age. Within the next few days it gained confidence, and I was able to observe it from close by. It was still silver-gray and had as yet no horns, though it was almost as tall as the adult owls, only much more slender and fluffy. I called it Pumpum, an imitation of an owl's call.

Bundu adopted Pumpum, while Pfeifer and the grandmother bird chased off the fish eagles that were besieging the place. I helped by waving my arms and shouting at them to go away. They usually took off the instant they saw me approach, even though they must have realized that I could do them no harm from so great a distance. Pumpum was not only protected by Bundu, Pfeifer, the grandmother, and myself, but also by the two Colobus. If I was searching for the little owl, all I had to do was look for the more conspicuous monkeys.

One morning I was filming Pumpum sunning herself on the gable of the garage roof and Bundu on a tree close by. After a while she tried to turn around and, flapping her wings to balance herself, fell off. Luckily she landed in a bougainvillaea bush, and though she got entangled, she was not hurt. Instantly Bundu flew to her rescue. After two months both made a routine of calling for food not only after dark, but also at dawn before the fish eagles arrived.

One morning I gave them a mole rat, which Pumpum picked up within three feet of me, while Bundu walked about thirty feet away. Pumpum dragged the rat quickly to her and, swaying her head submissively, begged to be fed, but Bundu hopped still farther and even pecked Pumpum as she followed her. So Pumpum then flew into a tree together with her rat and was followed by Bundu. Meanwhile, Pfeifer and her mother hooted a duet to keep a fish eagle, who also seemed interested in the mole rat, at bay. Not until they had chased him out of view did Bundu and Pumpum eat the rat.

Usually all four owls perched high up in a tree close together for their siesta, obviously joining forces against the fish eagles, since one of them would never dare to attack four of these formidable owls.

Instead of taking advantage of her security, Pumpum gradually developed the habit of flying down to the lawn by herself at odd hours of the day in search of food. Bundu would watch every move, but she never joined in unless a fish eagle swooped down. Then instantly there would be a swish of feathers, and Bundu, Pfeifer, and the grandmother bird would dive at the intruder. To witness these large birds with widespread wings driving the fish eagle far across the lake was a spectacular sight.

Pumpum soon learned that she was safe from predatory birds either on the veranda roof or on the door leading into the enclosure. From there she often called for food. She seemed to have accepted me as second-best nanny to Bundu, for now she made her submissive hunger dance when I approached, which normally she did only to Bundu.

Pumpum developed rapidly into a great character. One day I found her sitting on the water sprinkler, getting a shower. She looked too funny on this perch; drenched to the bone, her enormous black eyes seemed even larger than usual. On another occasion the cook announced that Pumpum was perching on a chair on the veranda, as if expecting to be served tea.

Next day she ventured farther into the house and sat on the dining room table. Luckily the large doors and windows are always open, so she could fly out without hurting herself. Later she made straight for the birdbath, a little pool in the center of the garden which is fed by a jet. Birds had sometimes hovered in the spray during the hot hours, but Pumpum plunged right into the water, ducking and preening herself. She seemed to enjoy the bath, and when she emerged, she looked ridiculous but very happy.

Pumpum was most endearing, and all the staff liked her. She seemed to regard me as a friend who was there entirely for her benefit. Not only did she find me at all times during the day if she felt hungry, with the exception of midday hours when she

72

snoozed, but even during the night I would hear her calling, although she had eaten plenty of food.

I cannot explain why she became more tame than any of the other owls, for she had known me for a much shorter time and much later in her life than Pfeifer and Bundu.

By 1979 our owl family had increased by nine offspring. It was most interesting to observe that the teamwork was repeated with every new chick: the mother confined herself to the protective role and left the feeding of the chick to the owlet who had last hatched and who was by then old enough to hunt. The task of the father seemed to be restricted to multiplying the family, without any further obligation to see to their welfare.

I never see more than four owls at Elsamere at the same time, and I assume the rest are incubating some distance away. It is most gratifying to know that all these owls are living free and that not one of them is dependent on my help for feeding, though when I call them by their names to offer them food they fly in from long distances and show the same trust in me they had when they were defenseless chicks. I am very fond of these magnificent owls and proud that they have made Elsamere their home.

POSTSCRIPT

Readers will wish to know what has happened to Elsamere since Joy Adamson's tragic death. The house
has been leased to the East African Power & Light-
ing Company for the use of their engineering staff
working on the Geothermal Power Project in Hell's
Gate. At the moment, an Indonesian couple are
staying at Elsamere; they have observed that a new
baby has recently been born to the Colobus monkeys, and that the owls are also still in residence.